INSULTS & COMEBACKS
SOCIALIST EDITION

Socialist in Silk - The Satire of Affluent Advocates | Mocking the Mismatch: Wealthy Warriors of Working-Class Woes

Jax Joust

Published by Lazy Cotton Press

PREFACE

Esteemed Readers,

Welcome to the sardonically sumptuous pages of "Insults and Comebacks - Socialist Edition: Socialist in Silk." In this volume, we dive into the delightful dichotomy of affluent advocates championing socialist ideals, weaving a tapestry of satire that playfully mocks the mismatch between high-society rhetoric and working-class realities.

This book isn't a critique of socialism itself but a humorous jab at its silk-stockinged spokespersons. We explore the ironic world of champagne socialists, from lecterns in ivy-covered towers to protests staged from penthouses, highlighting the incongruities in their well-meaning but often misplaced advocacy.

As you leaf through these pages, prepare for a journey filled with laughter, irony, and a bit of eye-rolling amusement. Whether you're a skeptic of high-flying socialists or a curious observer, this collection offers a light-hearted look at the complexities and contradictions of advocating for the working class while sipping artisanal coffee.

So, don your finest faux-fur-trimmed Che Guevara t-shirt and settle into your ergonomic, eco-friendly armchair; you're about to embark on an expedition that's as entertaining as it is enlightening, through the world of affluent socialist advocacy.

With a satirical smile and a raised eyebrow,

Jax Joust
2301 Lady Bug Drive, New York NY
November 2023

CONTENT

1 - The Well-Walled Socialists	1
2 - The Cafeteria Socialists	12
3 - The Strike Supporters' Paradox	23
4 - The Ivory Tower Revolutionaries	34
5 - The Champagne Marxists	45
6 - The Armchair Activists	56
7 - The Convenient Socialists	67
8 - The Digital Age Delusionists	78
9 - The Hypocrisy of the Mass Revolution Waiters	89
10 - The Misinterpreters of Marx	100

1 - The Well-Walled Socialists

In this chapter, we dive into the amusing irony of self-labeled socialists who, despite their loud advocacy for the working class, have rarely, if ever, had a meaningful conversation with an actual worker or peasant. Sheltered by their financial and social barriers, they romanticize a life they don't understand, blissfully unaware of the potential reception their idealistic notions might receive from those they claim to champion.

"You talk about the proletariat, but the closest you've come to a factory is a craft beer brewery tour."

"Your idea of interacting with the working class is asking your barista for an organic latte."

"You preach workers' rights but wouldn't last a day in their shoes – or work boots, rather."

"For someone who claims to stand with the workers, you sure stand a long way from them."

"You're like a zoo visitor talking about wildlife conservation – well-meaning but woefully removed from the reality."

"Your understanding of the working class is as deep as your last Uber driver conversation."

"You champion the cause of the workers, yet you wouldn't recognize one if they served you dinner."

"You romanticize the struggle of the working class but can't handle a Wi-Fi outage."

"To you, 'solidarity with the workers' means retweeting a hashtag from your latest-model smartphone."

"You speak of workers' revolutions, but the only thing you've ever led is a discussion group in your college's coffee shop."

2 - The Cafeteria Socialists

Focusing on those who preach socialism in university cafeterias but live a life far removed from socialist ideals, highlighting the irony of their privileged lifestyles clashing with their proclaimed beliefs.

"Advocating for the proletariat between sips of overpriced lattes – the height of cafeteria socialism."

"Their revolution starts and ends at the coffee shop – revolutionaries until the bill comes."

"Mistaking a heated debate over vegan options for class struggle."

"In the cafeteria, every socialist finds their voice, but loses it on the way to their air-conditioned dorm."

"Preaching about labor rights while the cafeteria staff clears their table – irony lost on the privileged."

"Wearing Che Guevara t-shirts, yet can't spell 'guerrilla warfare.'"

"Their idea of a class struggle is fighting for a seat in the campus café."

"They'll redistribute wealth, but not their untouched food to the homeless outside."

"Their manifesto is well-rehearsed, but only ever recited to fellow latte enthusiasts."

"Socialism for them is a trendy topic, as changeable as the campus fashion."

3 - The Strike Supporters' Paradox

Exploring the dilemma of students who support striking teachers, unaware of the irony in wasting their (or their parents') tuition money, which makes no real impact on the institution.

"Championing faculty strikes with the zeal of a revolutionary, blissfully ignorant of their wasted tuition dollars."

"Proudly marching with striking teachers, not seeing the tuition money burning in their wake."

"Their solidarity ends where their convenience begins – striking professors are heroes until exams are postponed."

"They'll support a strike, but ask them to sacrifice their grades? Suddenly, it's complicated."

"Solidarity with the strike, until it clashes with their spring break plans."

"They stand with striking staff, yet can't stand the thought of a delayed graduation."

"Enthusiastic strike supporters, until they realize their semester might be extended."

"Advocates for the workers, but only until it impacts their academic calendar."

"They want to change the world, but won't accept a change in their class schedule."

"Their activism is passionate, but evaporates when personal inconvenience looms."

4 - The Ivory Tower Revolutionaries

Criticizing teachers and academics who advocate for socialism while enjoying comfortable salaries and tenure, teaching subjects with little real-world job prospects for their students.

"Lecturing about proletariat struggles from the comfort of their ivory towers and tenured positions."

"Academics preaching socialism, blissfully insulated from the economic realities they discuss."

"Their socialist utopia fits perfectly in a world where job prospects and student debt don't exist."

"Promoting class struggle theories in classrooms more expensive than a worker's annual salary."

"They'll critique capitalism in a lecture hall, then cash their paycheck without a hint of irony."

"Teaching about wealth distribution, but none about the distribution of their six-figure salaries."

"Their socialism lectures are compelling, until you see the price tag of their course books."

"Eager to discuss labor exploitation, less keen on discussing their summer break in Tuscany."

"They shape young revolutionaries, but can't shape a realistic budget."

"Professors in socialism,
yet strangely comfortable in their
capitalist-funded institutions."

5 - The Champagne Marxists

Mocking those who claim to be socialists but lead lifestyles that contradict the core principles of socialism, enjoying luxury and capitalism's fruits while preaching revolution.

"Sipping champagne while lamenting the plight of the working class – a masterclass in Marxist hypocrisy."

"They toast to socialism with expensive wine, in apartments their working-class 'comrades' can't afford."

"Marx would turn in his grave at the sight of their designer clothes and luxury vacations."

"Preaching income equality, yet their wardrobes scream income excess."

"They talk of proletariat struggles from their gentrified neighborhoods, far from proletarian life."

"Their brand of socialism conveniently forgets the 'no luxury items' clause."

"They'd redistribute wealth, but not the kind that funds their lifestyles."

"Luxury cars and designer bags – the essentials for today's champagne socialist."

"In the world of practical socialism, they're more bourgeois than they'd ever admit."

"They dream of a socialist revolution, but won't part with a single luxury to fund it."

6 - The Armchair Activists

Highlighting the laziness of modern 'socialists' who believe sharing a post on social media is equivalent to meaningful political activism.

"Their revolution is fierce, until it involves leaving the comfort of their armchair."

"Leading the charge against capitalism, one online petition at a time."

"Their activism peaks at sharing a post – the digital age's version of a protest march."

"Passionate about change, as long as it doesn't require standing up."

"Their fight against the system is waged from the comfort of their living room."

"In the trenches of social media,
they battle injustice one like at a time."

"They'll change the world, right after this episode ends."

"Their commitment to the cause is as deep as their latest Netflix binge."

"They wear their social media activism like a badge, but it's more of a sticker."

"For them, 'struggle' is when the Wi-Fi is slow during their online protest."

7 - The Convenient Socialists

Focusing on individuals who adopt socialism as a fashionable label, treating it more as a trend than a commitment to actual societal change.

"Socialism is their fashion statement, worn and discarded like last season's trends."

"They embrace socialism like a designer label, to be shown off but not fully understood."

"Their socialism is as deep as their profile picture – a facade for likes."

"They'll wave the socialist banner, but only if it matches their aesthetic."

"Adopting socialism for its trendiness, not its tenets – the height of shallow conviction."

"Their idea of class struggle is deciding between Starbucks and local coffee."

"For them, socialism is just another accessory in their political wardrobe."

"They tout socialism at rallies,
but at home, it's capitalism as usual."

"Their commitment to socialism ends where real sacrifice begins."

"In their world, socialism is a social club, not a social responsibility."

8 - The Digital Age Delusionists

Addressing the failure of modern socialists to recognize how the digital age and internet economy have fundamentally altered the dynamics of labor, production, and ownership.

"They decry the exploitation of workers, yet tweet from smartphones made by underpaid labor."

"In their eyes, the digital revolution didn't change the socialist playbook – just added more hashtags."

"They bemoan capitalist exploitation, yet their entire platform relies on capitalist-created technology."

"Missing the irony of using tech platforms, the pinnacle of capitalist innovation, to preach socialism."

"For them, the digital age is just a backdrop for their outdated ideologies."

"In the era of tech startups, they're still preaching about factory floor uprisings."

"Their vision of socialism is as outdated as a dial-up connection in a fiber-optic world."

"They rail against the ills of capitalism using tools only possible in a capitalist system."

"In their narrative, Silicon Valley and Karl Marx somehow coexist in harmony."

"They use the digital economy to preach socialism, ignorant of the contradiction."

9 - The Hypocrisy of the Mass Revolution Waiters

Satirizing those who excuse their non-socialist behavior by claiming they're waiting for a mass revolution before they practice what they preach.

"Waiting for the mass revolution, but in the meantime, they're just fine with bourgeois comforts."

"They call for a revolution, but only after they finish their gourmet meal."

"Their revolution is always 'coming,' but never arriving – convenient for maintaining their lifestyle."

"They preach about the proletariat uprising, from the safety of their gentrified neighborhoods."

"Waiting for the world to turn socialist, but until then, their capitalist indulgences continue."

"They speak of revolutionary change, but their actions suggest they're quite comfortable with the status quo."

"For them, socialism is a future event, not a present commitment."

"They're revolutionary in theory, but in practice, they're decidedly status quo."

"They await a socialist utopia,
but won't lift a finger to create it."

"Their revolution has an indefinite start date – conveniently after their next luxury vacation."

10 - The Misinterpreters of Marx

Poking fun at the misinterpretation and oversimplification of Marxist theory to suit personal agendas or to appear intellectually sophisticated.

"Marx's words in their mouths are like pearls before swine – wasted and misunderstood."

"They quote Marx like gospel, yet their understanding is less Das Kapital, more comic strip."

"Marx would be less 'Das Kapital' and more 'Das Katastrophe' with their interpretations."

"They use Marxism like a Swiss Army knife – versatile in theory, ineffective in practice."

"Their grasp of Marxist theory is as tenuous as their grip on reality."

"Wielding Marx's theories like a toddler with a hammer – everything looks like a nail."

"For every complex problem, they have a simple solution, courtesy of a misread Marx quote."

"Marx in their hands is less revolutionary and more a tool for social posturing."

"They think they understand Marx, but they can't even understand the contradictions in their lifestyles."

"In the library of socialism,
they've read the cover of Marx's work,
but none of the pages."

EPILOGUE

Dear Discerning Reader,

As we close the gilded cover of "Insults and Comebacks - Socialist Edition," we find ourselves at the end of an amusing and thought-provoking journey. This tome has been more than a collection of clever comebacks; it's been a satirical exploration into the world of socialist advocacy as seen through the lens of affluence.

Throughout these pages, we've navigated the paradoxical terrain of wealthy warriors for the working class. We've chuckled at their well-intentioned but often misguided efforts, pondering the irony of advocating for the masses from the comfort of luxury.

Remember, the jibes and jests contained within are not merely for amusement; they're a light-hearted probe into the nuances of advocating for change while ensconced in comfort. As you move forward, armed with this anthology of witty retorts, use it to spark dialogue, to challenge perceptions, and to appreciate the delicate dance between ideals and reality.

As we part ways, may your path be graced with insightful encounters and your conversations be as rich in substance as in humor. Until our next foray into the realm of witty repartee, I bid you farewell, hoping your days are filled with as much meaningful action as they are with laughter.

With a bemused nod and a gentle jest,

Jax Joust
November 2023

© 2023 by Lazy Cotton

All rights reserved. No part of this publication may be reproduced, distributed, or transmitted in any form or by any means, including photocopying, recording, or other electronic or mechanical methods, without the prior written permission of the author, except in the case of brief quotations embodied in critical reviews and certain other noncommercial uses permitted by copyright law.

First Edition

Published by Lazy Cotton Press
www.lazycotton.press

Published by Lazy Cotton Press
www.lazycotton.press

Printed in Great Britain
by Amazon